HE INTERCOURSE

DAVID RAFAEL WANG

the greenfield review press
greenfield center ny

Acknowledgements:

Sumac
the goodly co
Trace
Original Works (England)
Greenfield Review
Light Up
The Invisible City
New Directions ⧣ 19
Nomad
Galley Sail Review
Venture

TO
Trautmann Gregory Witte
and
H. J. Tschirner,
wherever they are

G. R. Chapbook No. 18
ISBN 0-912678-18-6
Copyright D.R. Wang 1975

photos, cover and p. 33: Ron D'onofrio
drawings, p. 7 and p. 21: M.L. Brannock Lunde
photo of D.R. Wang: Roger B. Smith
design: Charlotte Cohen

We wish to express our thanks for the National
Endowment for the Arts, for a Small Press Grant
which has made the publication of this book possible.

Glad Day Press
UNION SHOP I.U. 450
308 Stewart Ave., Ithaca, N.Y. 14850

contents

act I
the thrusts

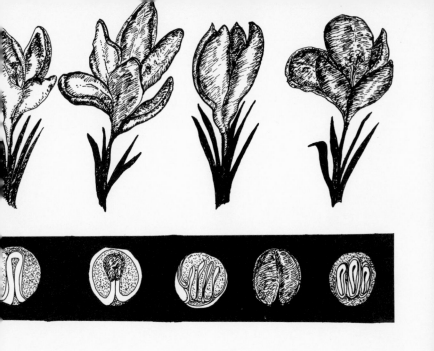

KOUROS

To capture your beauty:
Ring a gazelle tight with a rope
And watch him bound through the woods.

DYNAMO

The stately chief
who twirls his hands,
his feet stamping
in tune to the báte,
cannot shelter from
our sight the lithe
Samoan boy, intense,
beating time on
a garbage can, his body
a rivulet of sweat
under the glaring light
of the crepe-ribboned stage.
A streamline flowing
from neck to legs,
He releases time
with the insistent rise
and fall of his hands,
as the heaving
of his chest unknots
the muscles of his
waist and back.

Music evolves
from his stance:
When the muscles
of the drummer stretch,
Our bodies sway.

THE NUANCES
(for Jeannie & Alan)

It is
all in the
unsaid,
all in the
vein that rises
smouldering,
crying out
like the young
boy, a
guitar strummed
for his girl
at the bottom
of the dark stairs
where across strings
and silences
beam the
gritty eyes of love.

THE WAVE

In the desert
you can see
waves of needles
stabbing thru the air.

They are real too—
sharper than the
cacti you can
touch and break.

What each one
touches
springs alive
to his hand.

THE SOLUTION

It is painful
as some say
to be united with none
beyond pairs of legs.

As for me
I don't care
whether they are
artificial or well-made.

If she lifts
her skirt I'll
dig a tunnel
to her head.

INTAGLIO
(for Filippo Pilace)

The crocus
　　that thrusts its
　　　stamen up in the air
　　　　has not a more independent stance
　　　　than when she bends to rub
　　　　　lotion over his sunburnt legs
　　　　his hardness waking
　　　　　　to the caress of her hand.

THE SHOCK

Looking at your
round mouth
around the corn,

I bit my lips
raw
just in time.

THE STAKE

Stay cool
        baby
                stay cool/ he says
     a boy of 18 or
                19/ if over a day
It's all your mind/ control
—that's where I'm ahead/ the only thing
       real is his/ not
                     the Beatle haircut or
                     blond locks of hair/ the
      white T-shirt or levi
                  also
                        other boys wear/ but
the flesh
       skin
           outthrusts
              the plain wear
declares:
       In my physique
               you see
                  the mind
reigns.

THE UNTAMED

My wife always figures:
   an expert performing on my lines
opening my eyes to the bloom
                of scattered panties & littered gowns
screaming "Help!" when none
                     is drowned
raising her melon face
              from a black book
        heavy with columns
        I Am
        You Is
        He Are
        We Writes
demanding that I rub her
        when my pen
                is cold to the sheet
                wrinkled, unironed
insisting that I put
        my rubbers on
        when the room wavers in a flood
                of morning light.
What my wife
        insisted, I have
tried, but when she opens
        her mouth, the poem
              slinks out.

TROBAR

The flower
that lives
but a day
opens its petals
to wilt
in your hand.

I would have
gladly
done the same
had you drenched me
in the sunlight of
your shade.

THE INARTICULATE
(for Richard Costello)

It is not the ut-
most joy to talk
to you when your
mind is more at-
tuned to mathematics
than poetry and art.

But to watch you
on the horizontal
bar, chinning up and
down and spinning
completely around, I
want to extend
to touch your bi-
ceps and expanding
wings but how my
heart /stops/ shy.

THE ASH-HAULER

Race never enters the picture
Superman has turned black
Let him flap his biceps
Swoop down upon the villains
See how fast they turn and run
dropping their used powder puffs

At least, the pasty-faces are scared stiff
to face a two-fisted panther
who doesn't need to snarl
to get his teeth to light up
in the sparkle of his sunny nature

If you don't get this, man, dig:
Us spade cats will shovel white trash
into the underground furnace of love.

act II
the insertions

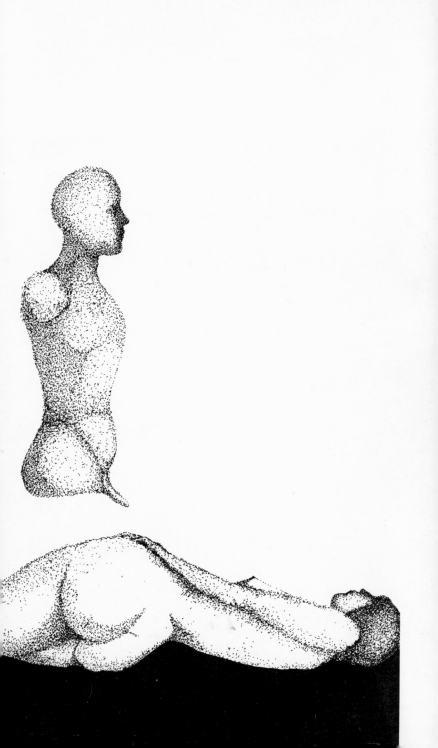

THE RUB
(for Sherrill & Jay)

Watching you wash him,
a small
washcloth held tight,
your hands going up
and down, rubbing Balmain
over his sweat
from armpits past navel
to his back, I see you
both on fire/ the bodies
in the concentration
of your mind/ the act
cuts thru the grease, the smudge
as the muscle
beneath his skin
extends & gathers light.

THE WOMAN

The courage
to follow your
instinct/ regardless/ to
have him carry you into
the bedroom/ then ask to be
left alone
              with him
barring me out/ to whom you've
proffered your friendship &
welcome/ is not just a door
slammed in my face

                        (the egotistic poet, not
                        even the modesty of a
                        cough)
                              but a slap with
a wet sheet to
revive my wonder at
your singleness, your dedication
to your man/ for which
words can never touch
all that is admirable in woman.

THE COVER

The skin is
vulnerable, tender,
all exposed, as you've
opened to me your
mind, not your heart.

What's more natural for you
than to cry out as
he covers your skin with
his and turns off
the light?

THE RITE

—for my wife

To be gentle
is a hardship:
the strain
to bend, to twist
your muscle to open the
wound without
breaking tissues
to reach the
recess and warm up
the ligaments

Such demands have
made saints shy
away from the
ritual/ to prefer the ecstasy
of extinction to the
rigors of constant
glow/ to hold back
just in time before it
burns thru

But weaker than saints/ let's
throw in the
candle and watch the taper
melt as the heart
grows bold.

THE YIELDING

My wife holds
mine and puts
it in her mouth. This act
of sharing can
not be described.

Let your wife
do the same
and see if you
can resist
when she tries.

THE INTERCOURSE

You've been having
   sex with her
   four times a day
But with me
   once only
   in life you have. . .
I should be
   jealous, but, no,
I can't/ You can fill
   her up when
   her body spreads
But with me nothing
   changed even if you
came/ we could be in bed
   again & again/ but
at best, it will be
   simulated sex: only cocks
   & pussies
         are strangely
matched - I turned to you
for your whole being, not just your arms,
                your buttocks,
                your legs/ only
   when I watch the light
spreading over your face
   when I stray into
   what we have shared:
          pot, jazz, Greek gods, nymphets, &
          ideas/ do
we come
   to a collaboration of wills, with
   cold sheet transmuted into
     scroll of words
       more urgent & intense
         than the ruffled bed.

THE CROSS

The filthy
thought of all three
of us in the same bed
making it
would churn the
stomach of our Puritan fathers, of
which—thank god—I have none
to boast.

　　　　The link of
desire would burn thru
to sear our bed upside
down into
a statute of love.

THE BREAK

These things are not to be
written in a book
what we did together
in your room
behind the closed door the
words you used
are matched by the lights
we turned off
to see them glow. All
words are second to the
act/ all acts second to
what you will do. When you
break down, my light goes
out, but words leap
sudden to my throat.

OUT IN HOLLYWOOD

#1 The Dare
Sitting on a fire hydrant,
He taunts passing motorists:
             "Hi, faggot!"

#2 Collision
One thin T-shirt worn at the seams,
Pair of tight jeans hugging his crotch,
He sticks out his thumb to hitch a ride.

Two cars lose control
And land by his side.

#3 Progress Report
At ten he admired
             Tarzan's physique.

At fifteen he worked-
             out like Steve Reeves.

Now in his twenties he sells
             his buns all week.

#4 Double Exposure
Obsessed with sex acts,
He never gets a hard-on.
Ranting against cardinal sin,
He got caught with pants down.

#5 The Tumescence
One would imagine him
the Golden Boy of
hitchhiking as he offers
himself at $35 a night in ex-
change for a ride on Sunset Blvd.

The waves where he
body surfs off Santa Monica
must be swelling with gold
as he mounts them in the heat
of midday sun.

#6 Bike Boy
With your broad back bent,
kneeling on the ground,
you stroke the tubes
gently as you polish
it all around.

If you could
lavish this care
on your bike, how much
more could you have given
to the pregnant
one left behind?

7 Pacesetter
n All-American boy with only one exception:
le's slept with girls, lesbians, old men, and even an African queen.

8 Flower Power
At the sight of the semi-nude young Marine
The flamboyant queen can no longer contain excitement
Edging up to him and pulling off his shorts
(S)he inserts a flower up his rectum.

act III
the withdrawal

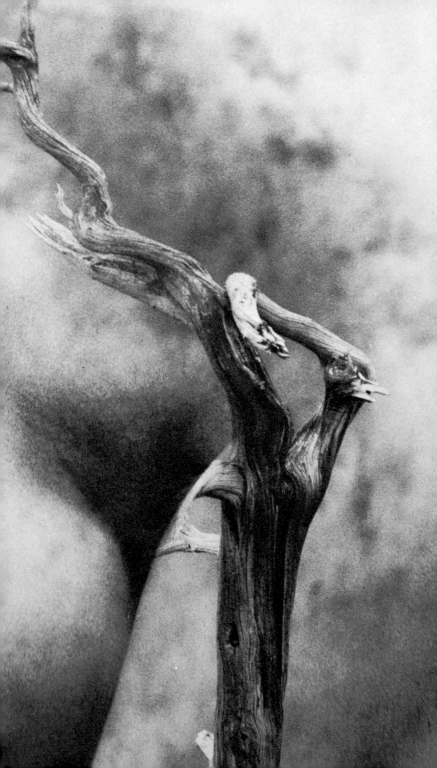

THE TRUCE

How can we
learn to share
what we like

in this world
where love's
often so contrived

that kisses
are to be
mixed with
ice-cubes in
a glass/ for her whose
skirt
is torn between
your husband's suspender
and your envious eyes?

How hard it is
to drop the layers
of dress all at
once and admit
the game is simply:
Cancel each other out

But I conceal no
weapon under the glare of
my maroon socks and
you can equally
let your ravenous dark
hair down/ before suspicion
snares and snips the wings
of the free-floating
jay, the plume
of our delight.

THE CONSEQUENCE

To trace the form
is to miss what's
under there
The velvety skin
hints only of
seething secrecy
betraying no more
than the smile that
illuminates his face
or the ripples that
rise and fall when
he heaves his chest
To search all the
mountains and ridges
would be in vain
to find an equation
when he bends his back
When he winks the moon
shines in his face
The ocean roars when
he steps out of the wave
When he basks the sun
touches him from
feet to head and giggles
transform the girls
when he strips on the sand
yet it would be far easier
to pronounce his name
to the wind that blows
in your face than trace
his form in the cooling
air that settles with the fog
over the San Francisco Bay
leaving Oklahoma a distant memory
to the Choctaws and Cherokees
who could never fore-
tell the consequence that
might break bread with you
today.

THE LAPSE

As long as you are
absorbed in scrubbing your neck,
with your blue shirt tied
unceremoniously around your waist
your bright looks make
Apollo almost look pale
But when you open
your mouth your nimbus
fades and you are
but another ranch-
hand washing his face.

COOL CAT
(for Gary Snyder)

The rain has soaked the cabin
The wind has shaken the mast
My mistress's red petticoat is wet
And knitted are the eyebrows of my lovely wife

I tie the boat to the nearest tree
And observe the flowering billows
The bamboo blinds are left sagging
The broken teacups litter the deck

On my way back I feel a sudden calmness:
Autumn has invaded the summer
I dry my sleeves in a Yoga posture
And leave the girls to fret and chatter.

A PRAYER FOR LUCRETIA
(per Aida Mastrangelo)

In glee the lady shakes his tree
And bares her soul to the naked beast,
Who blandly churns her gilded sea
With crescive skin of Sinai's peak,

Where Moses sells his book to Pan,
Where satyrs dance at Diane's feast,
Where Circe changes pigs to men
And Spartans turn delirious-meek;

Yet, lo! when Hermes has his play,
Wanton Cyclops spreads like yeast
Not in vials of ardent May
But in wine for Holy Week.

Oh, Christ, whose mother we shall be,
Grant us the folly to be free!

IN THE CITY

Where the worms are roasted
In their gaudy garments,
Where the sporty racedogs
Pride themselves
On the kingsized cartons
Of their phaloi,
With which they galavant
Up and down
The maidenforms,
A 'lonely young man'
Seeks in vain
For a skyscraper
To hang his heart on,
While
In the distance
There lingers
The ghost of a cathedral chime,
Beckoning tattered heathens
To manna of grace
Beyond the fruits of
Earthly wrongs,
Till it drives his head
Buzz, buzz, buzz,
In circles by an
Obscene fly,
Which drifts like melted ice cream
Down
A stained altar glass.

POEMS OF SEPARATION

I. Wei City Song
In the city of Wei
    morning rain dampens the dust
By the traveler's lodge
    greener and greener the willows grow

Let me persuade you
    to drain just one more cup
Once out of the Yang fortress
    There will be no friends.
                —Wang Wei (701-761)

II. Seeing Off at Bramble Gate
Traveling far to the Bramble Gate Mountain,
You came voyaging from the State of Ch'u.
The mountain sweeps down with the moor;
The river rushes into the wasteland.
Under the moon a heavenly mirror gyres
And clouds float, knotting an undersea palace.
Still thinking of the land and water of our home,
I see your sail depart for ten-thousand miles.
                —Li Po (701-762)

III. Bitter Parting
At fifteen I was engaged to you
At twenty I was carried through the gate
Once I have entered your gate
I find you constantly away
In the morning I see you off
In the evening I see you off again
If I snap you another willow branch,
The tree will soon collapse.
I'd sooner be the dirt on the road
Where your horse hooves could rest.
I'd sooner be the branch of a tree
To serve as the wheel of your carriage.
Could I but move the high mountain
And block the horse's advance!
                —Shao Yeh (late T'ang Dynasty)

SOUVENIR SHEET

In the end
it's all the
same: rolling
a cigarette or
rolling a
queer.

"The damn
fag," he sez
"wanted me to
piss in his/ well
I did and kicked
him in
the crotch for that/ how's
that."

A clean
act/ his hands
weren't even
stained:
nicotine/ fag, and
he rolled up
the sheet
from under
before he
started

"just a
souvenir," he
sez "for
me and my
broad/ man
Ain't got
nothin' better
than that."